TEACH ME, MAN

SERIES

BRANDS
OF THE
TRADE

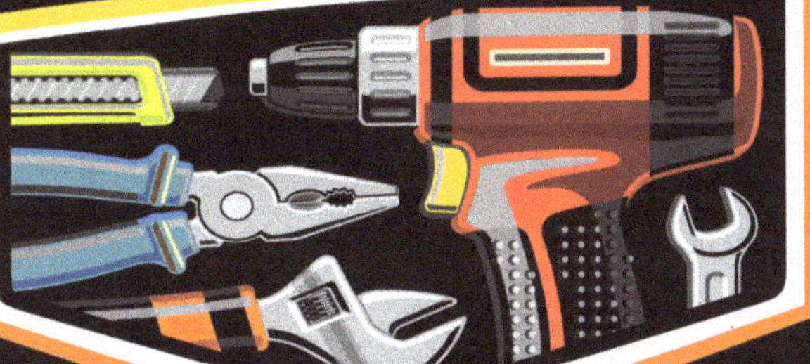

VOLUME 1

NATHAN SCOTT VALE

Milwaukee

FOR FATHERS EVERYWHERE...

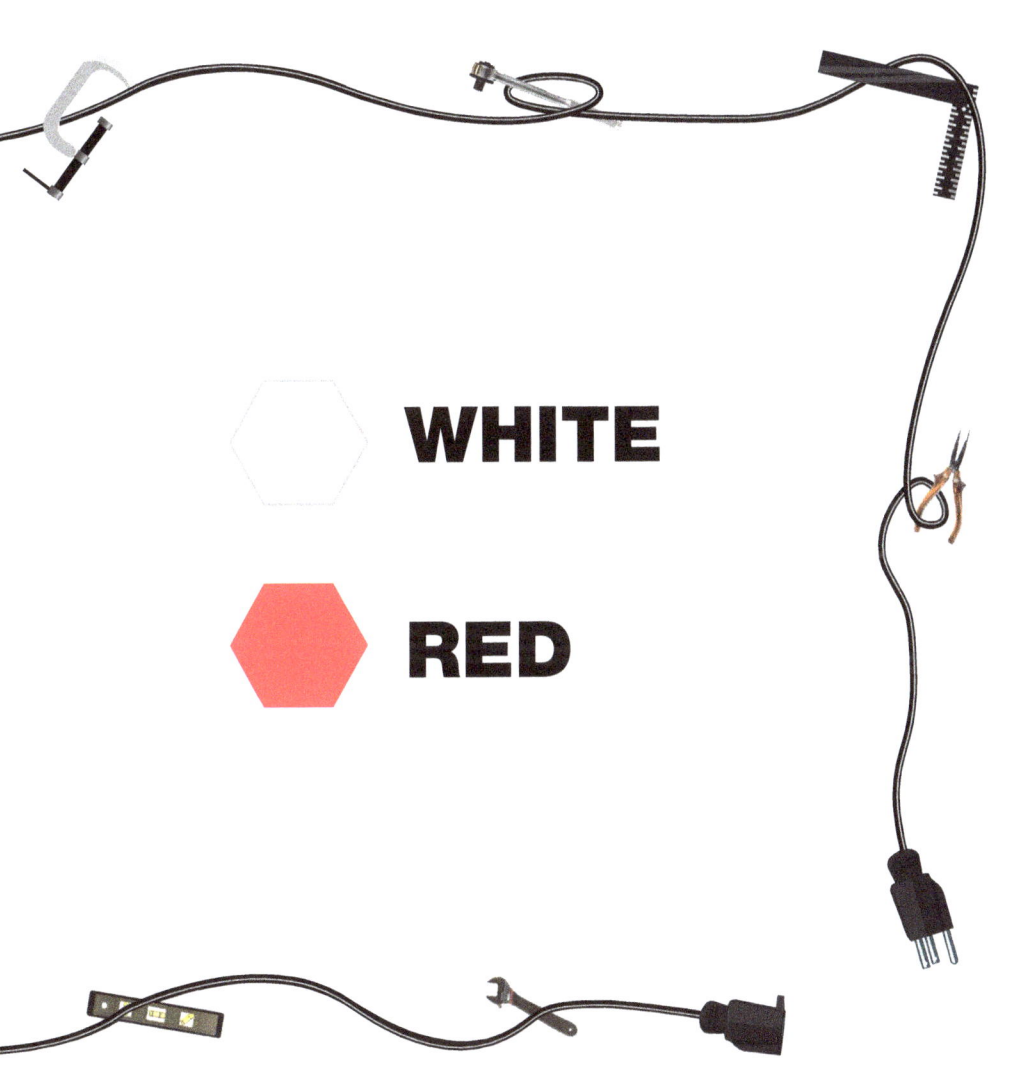

WHITE

RED

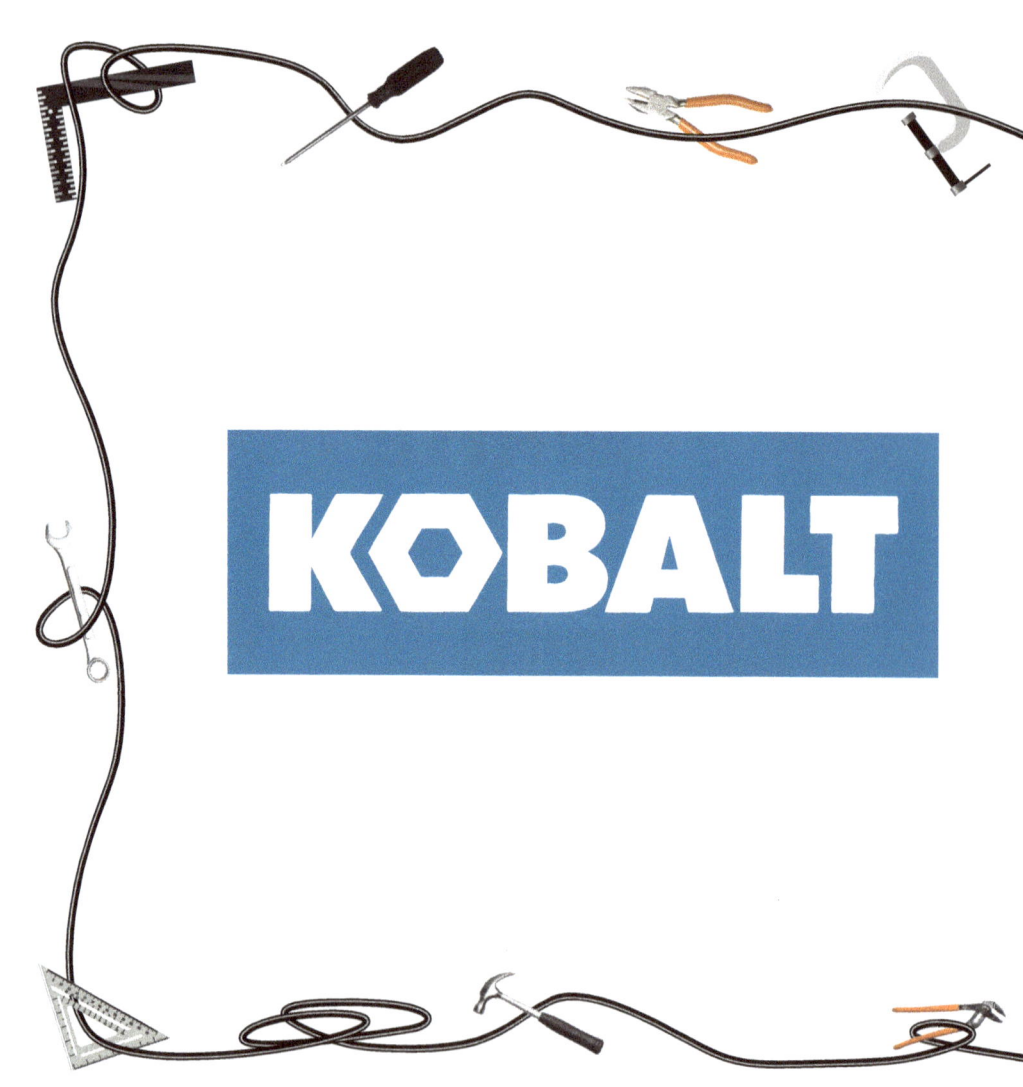

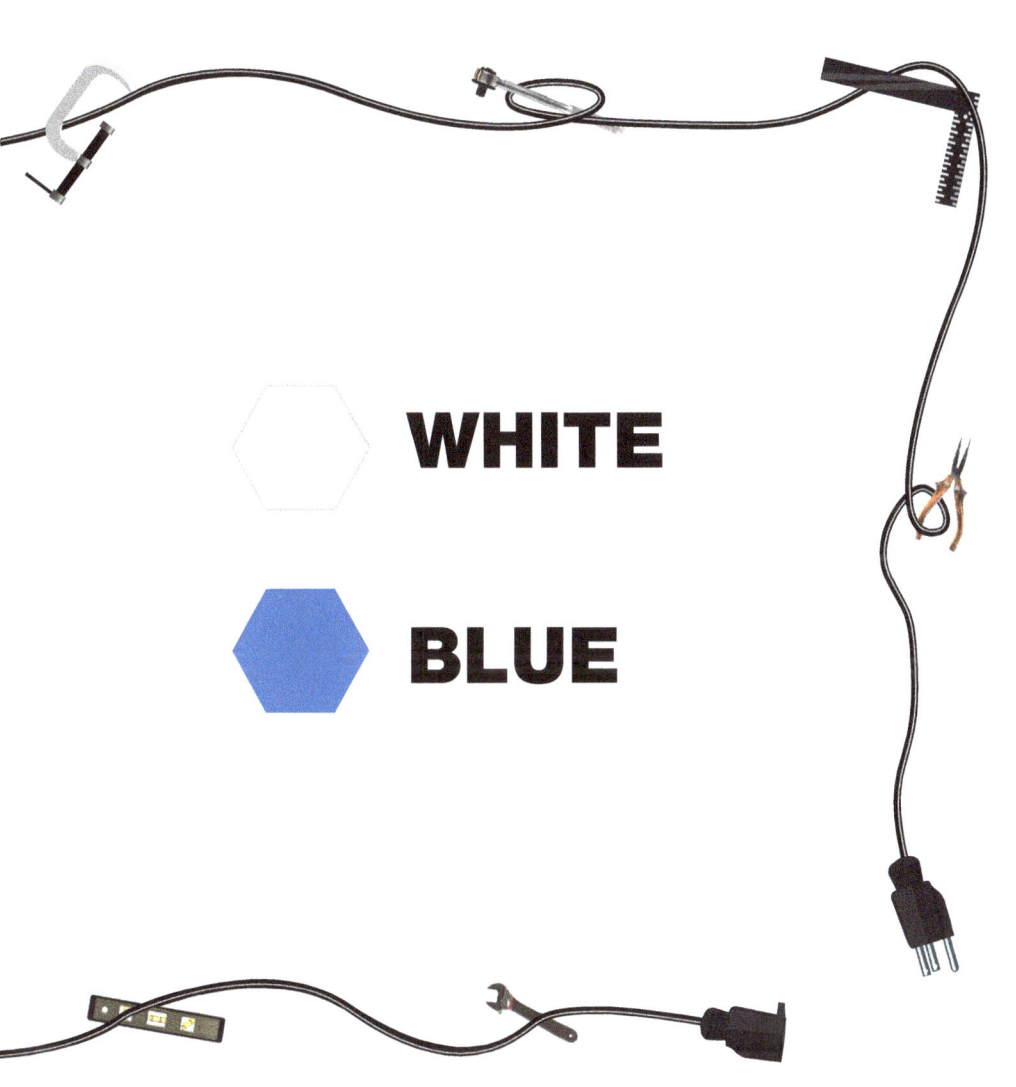

WHITE

BLUE

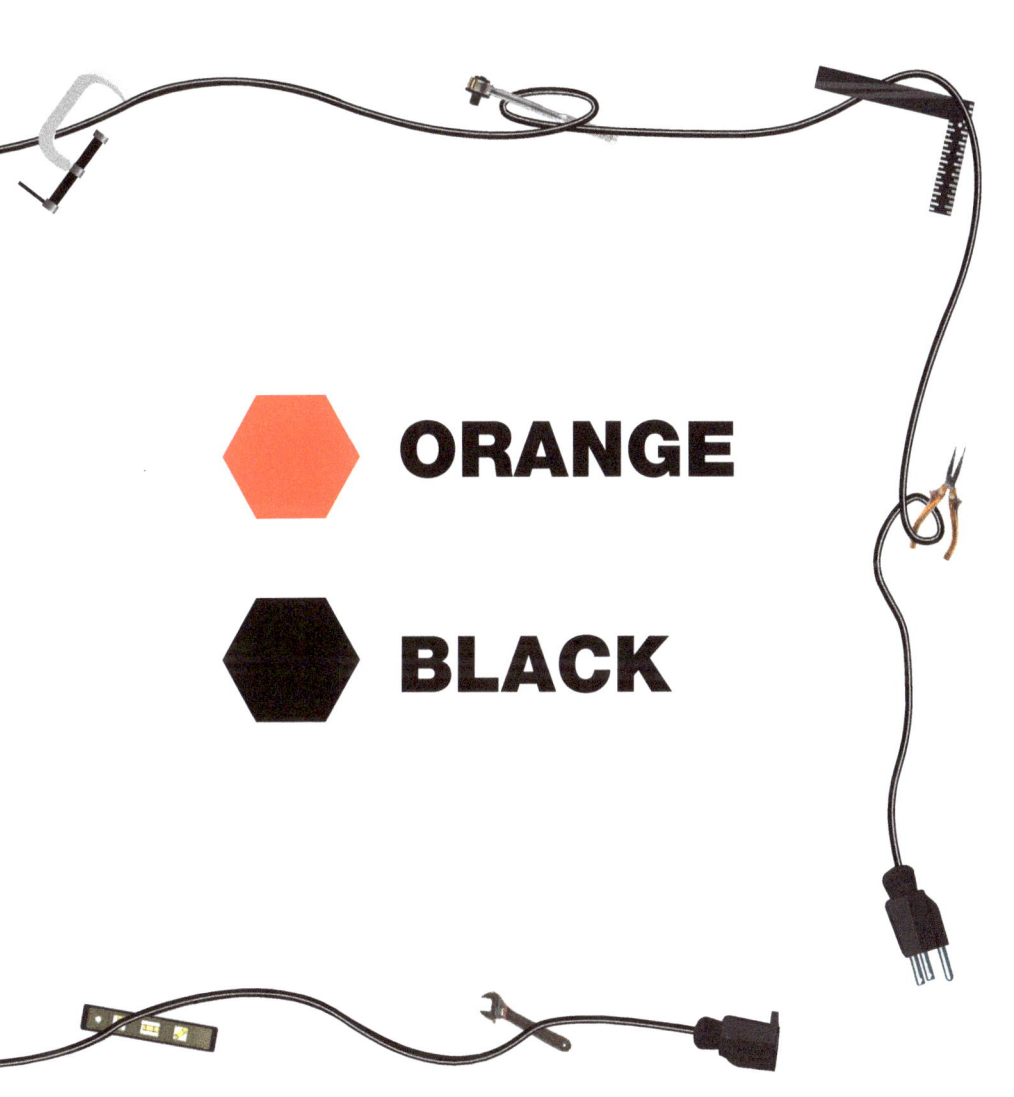

ORANGE

BLACK

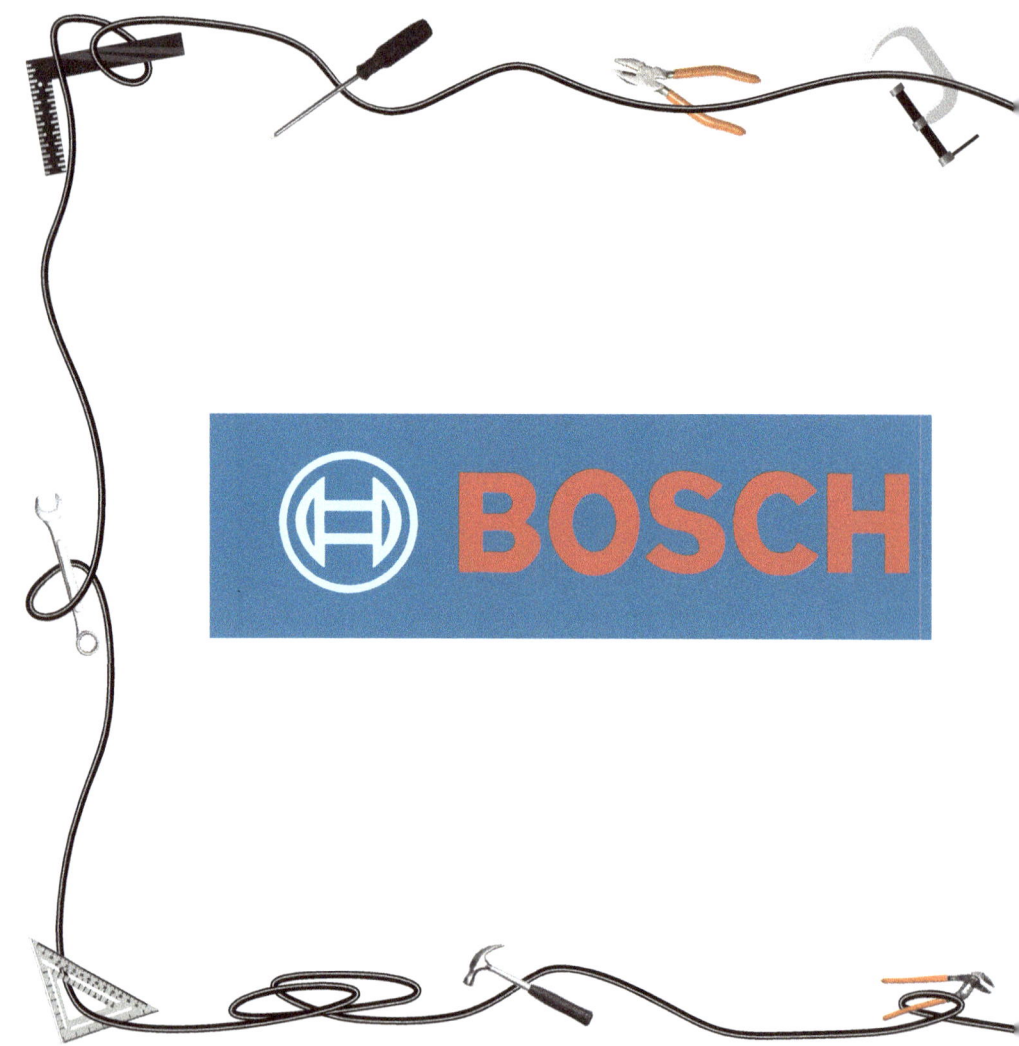

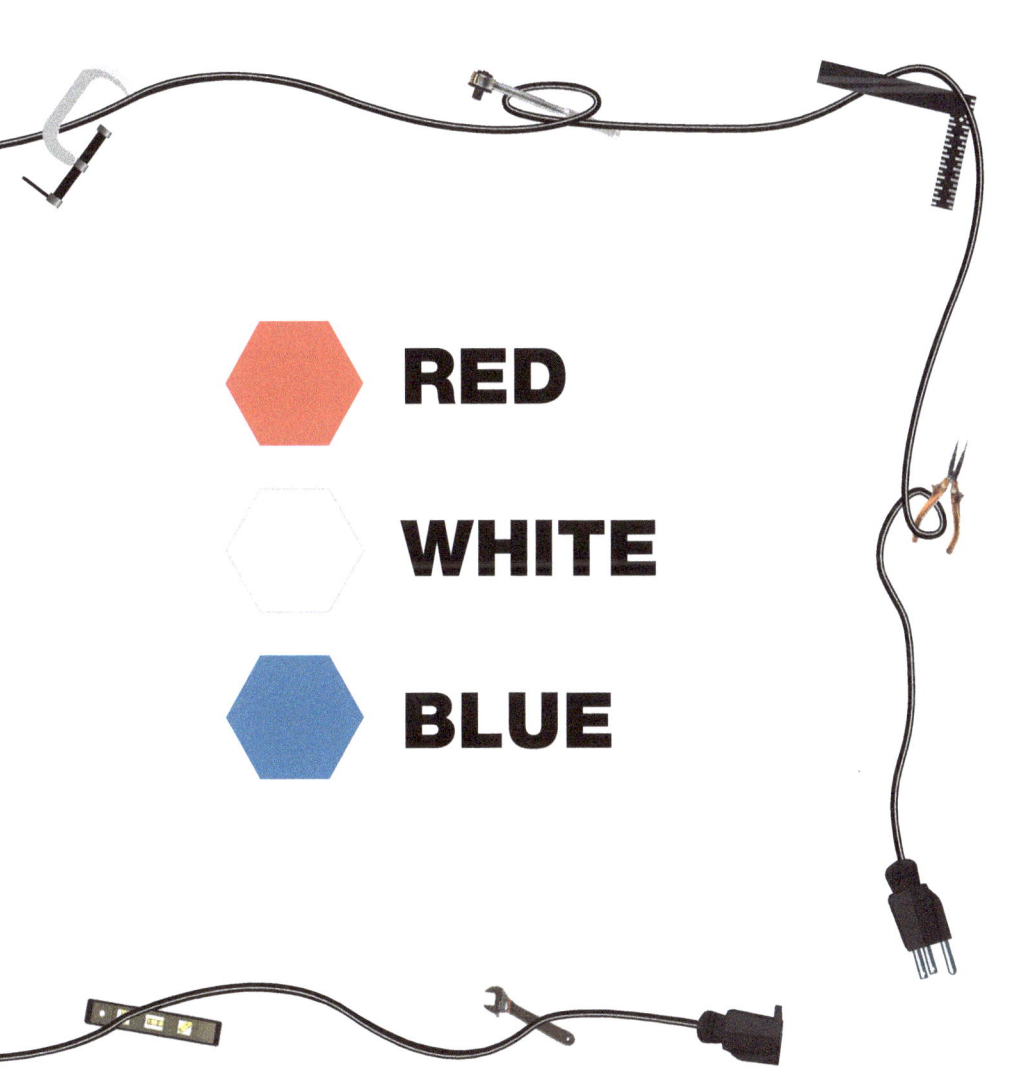

RED

WHITE

BLUE

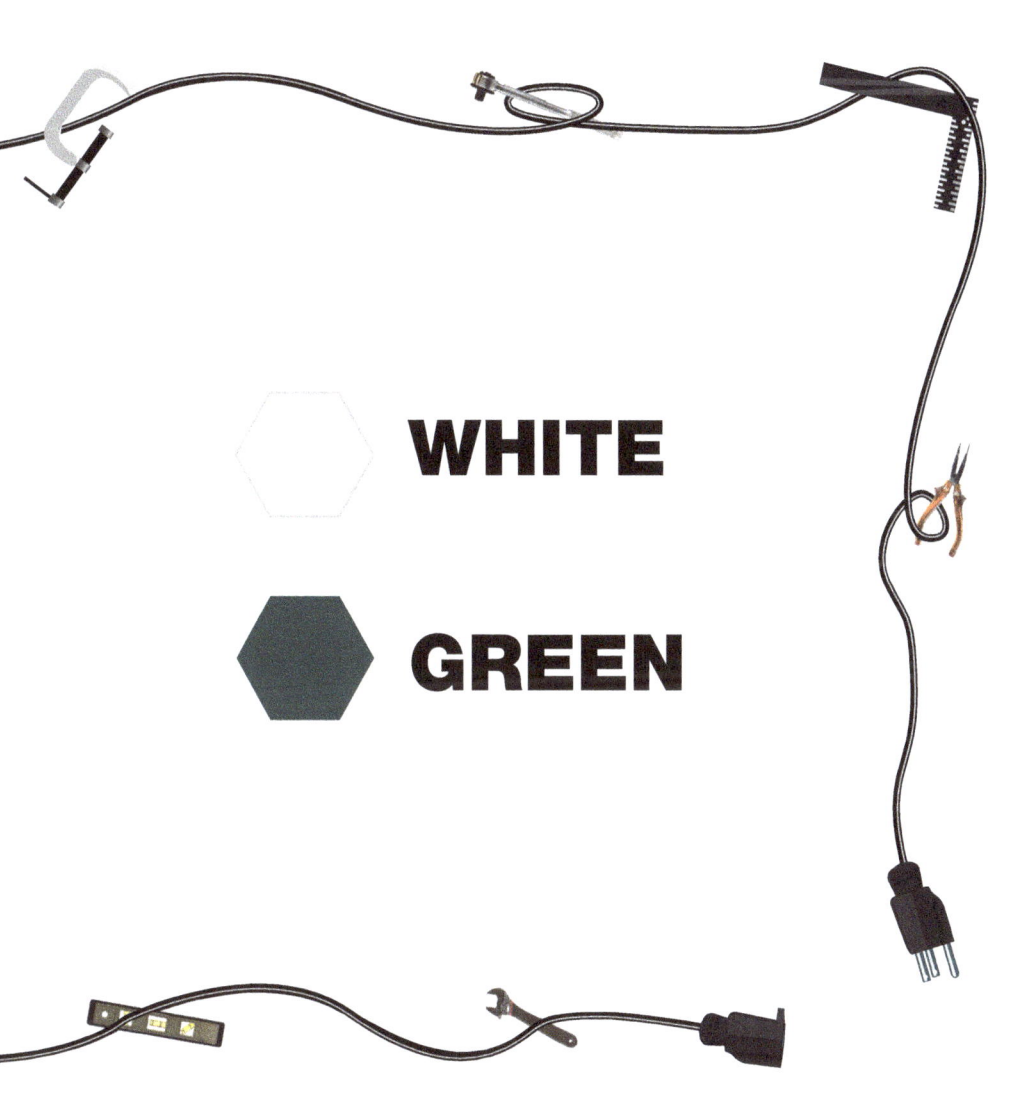

WHITE

GREEN

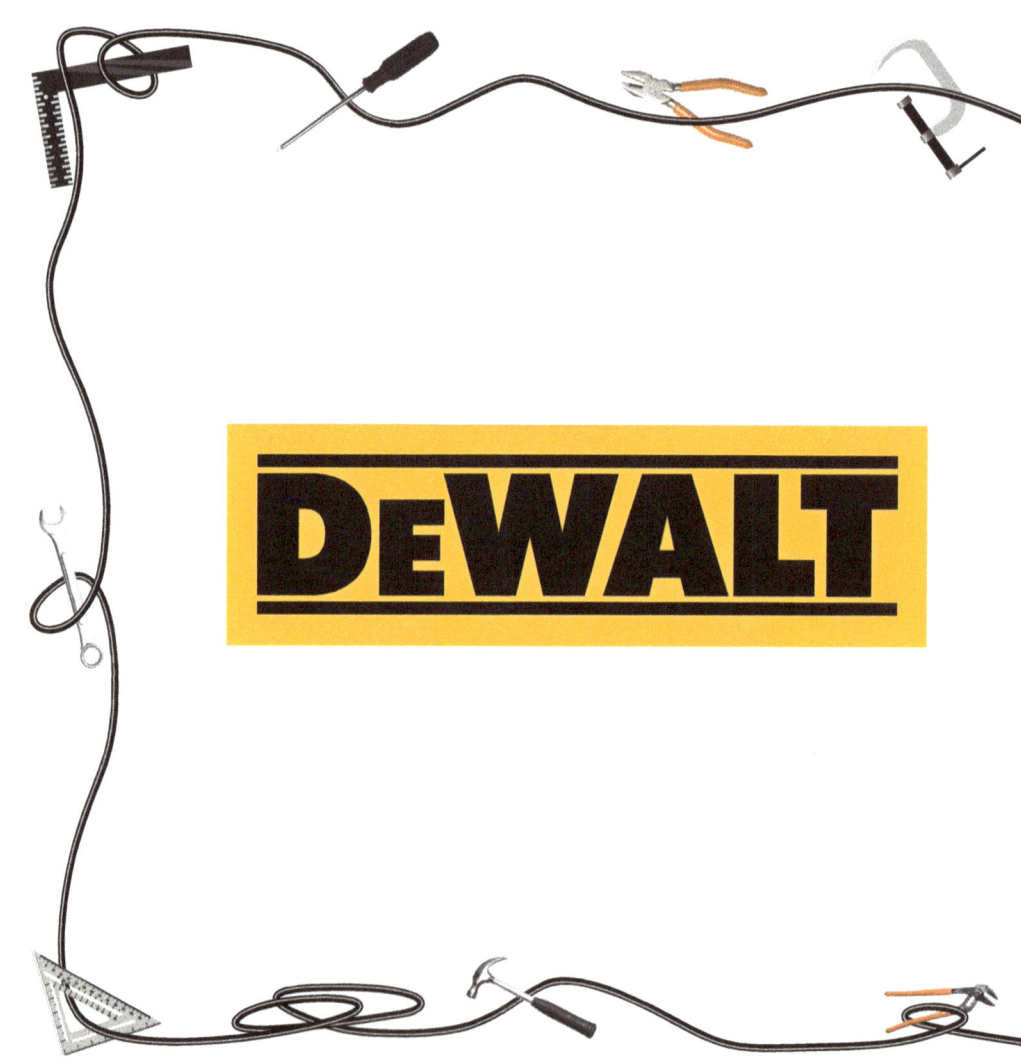

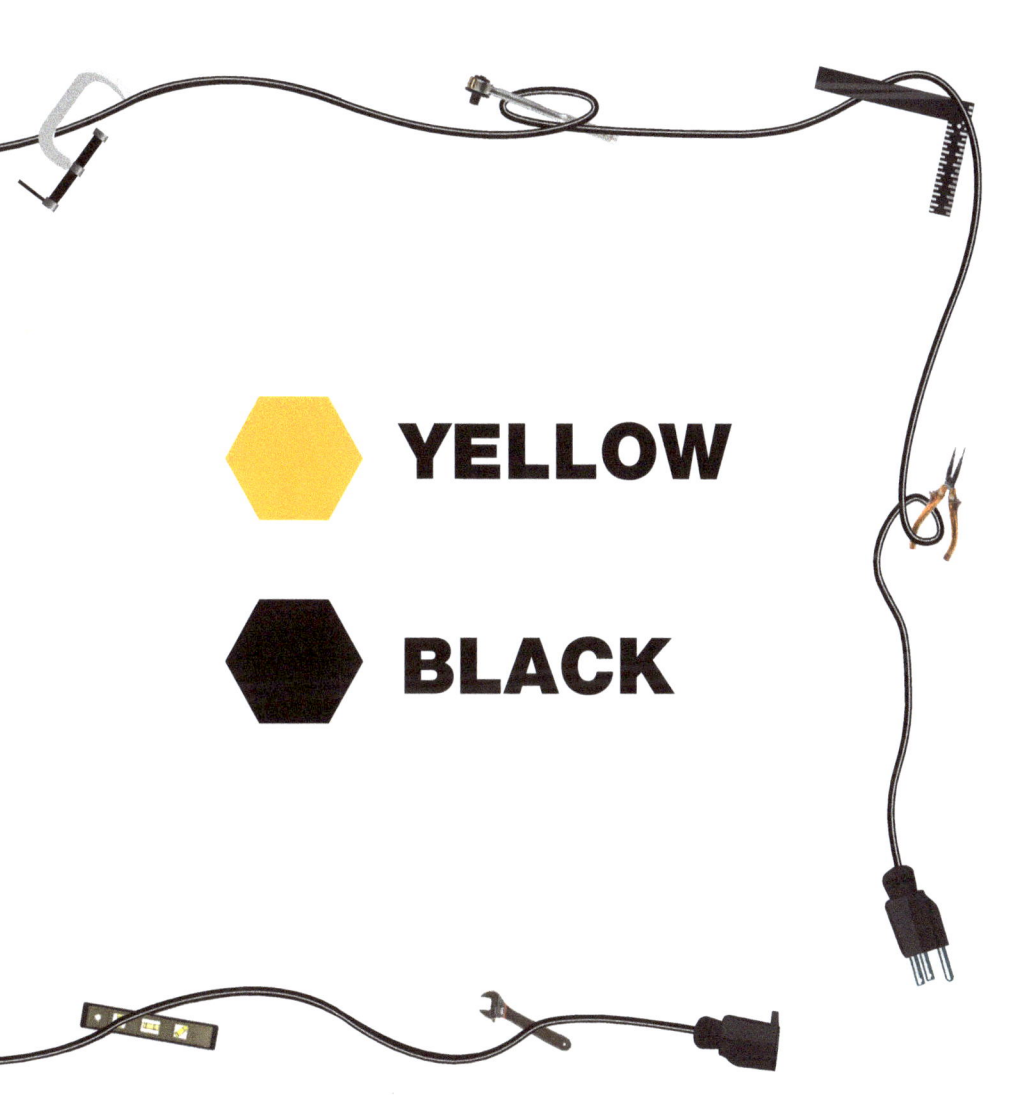

YELLOW

BLACK

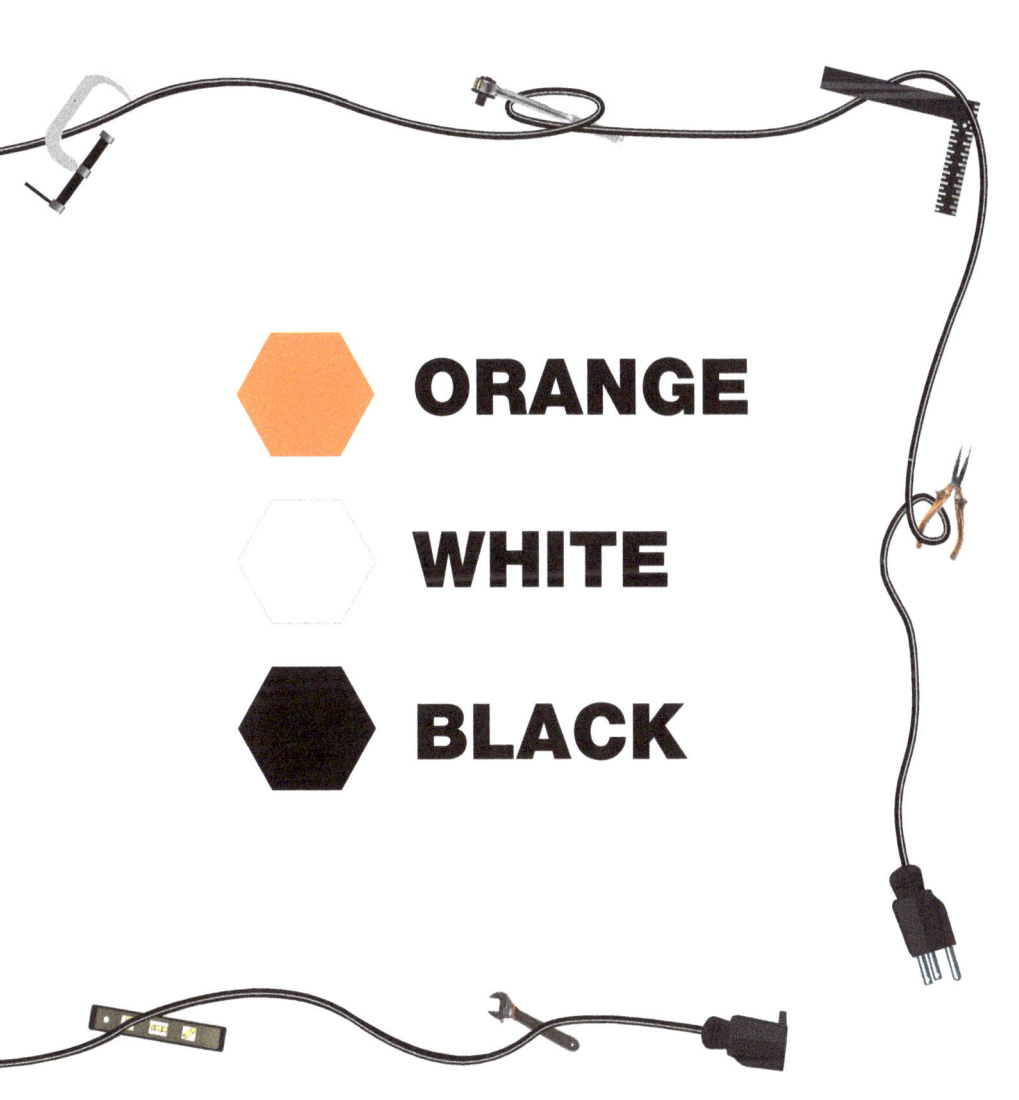

ORANGE

WHITE

BLACK

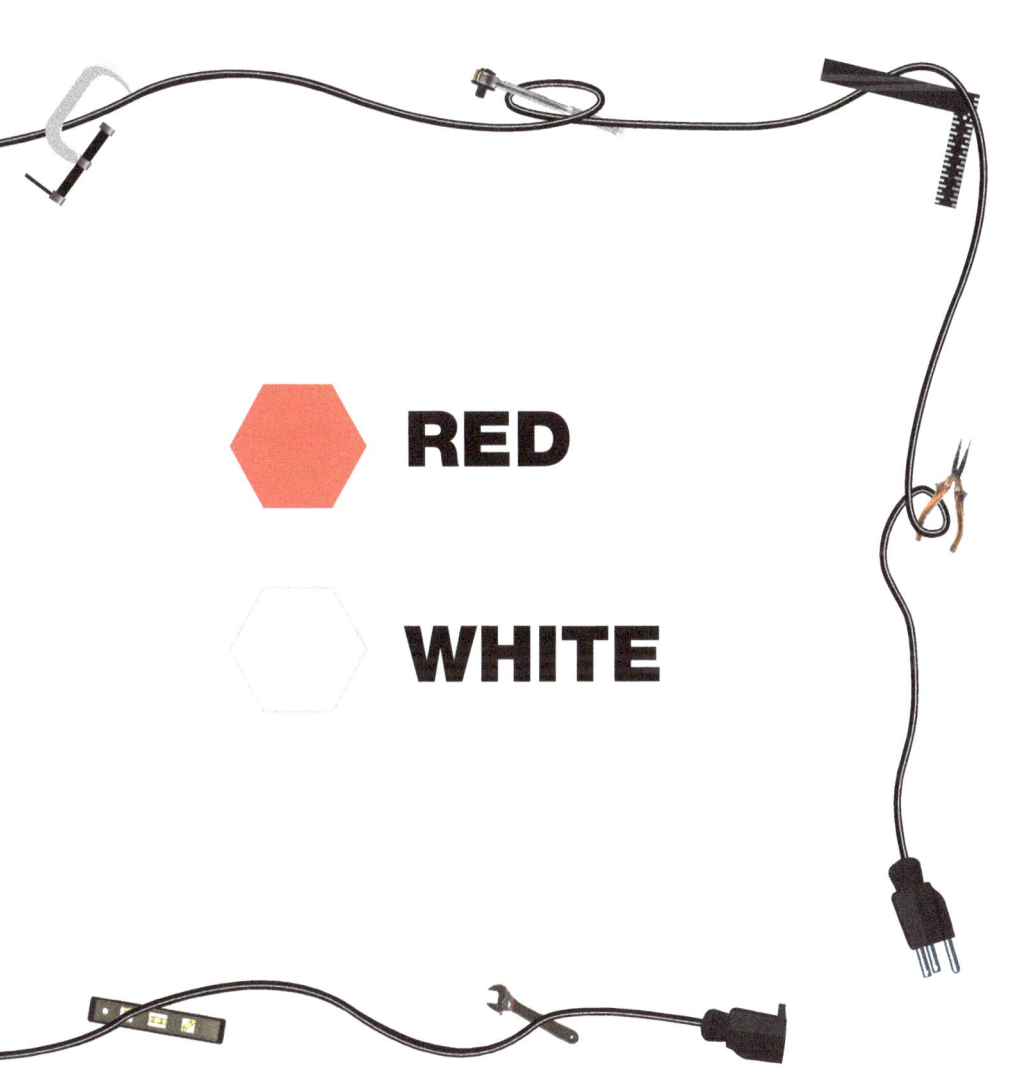

RED

WHITE

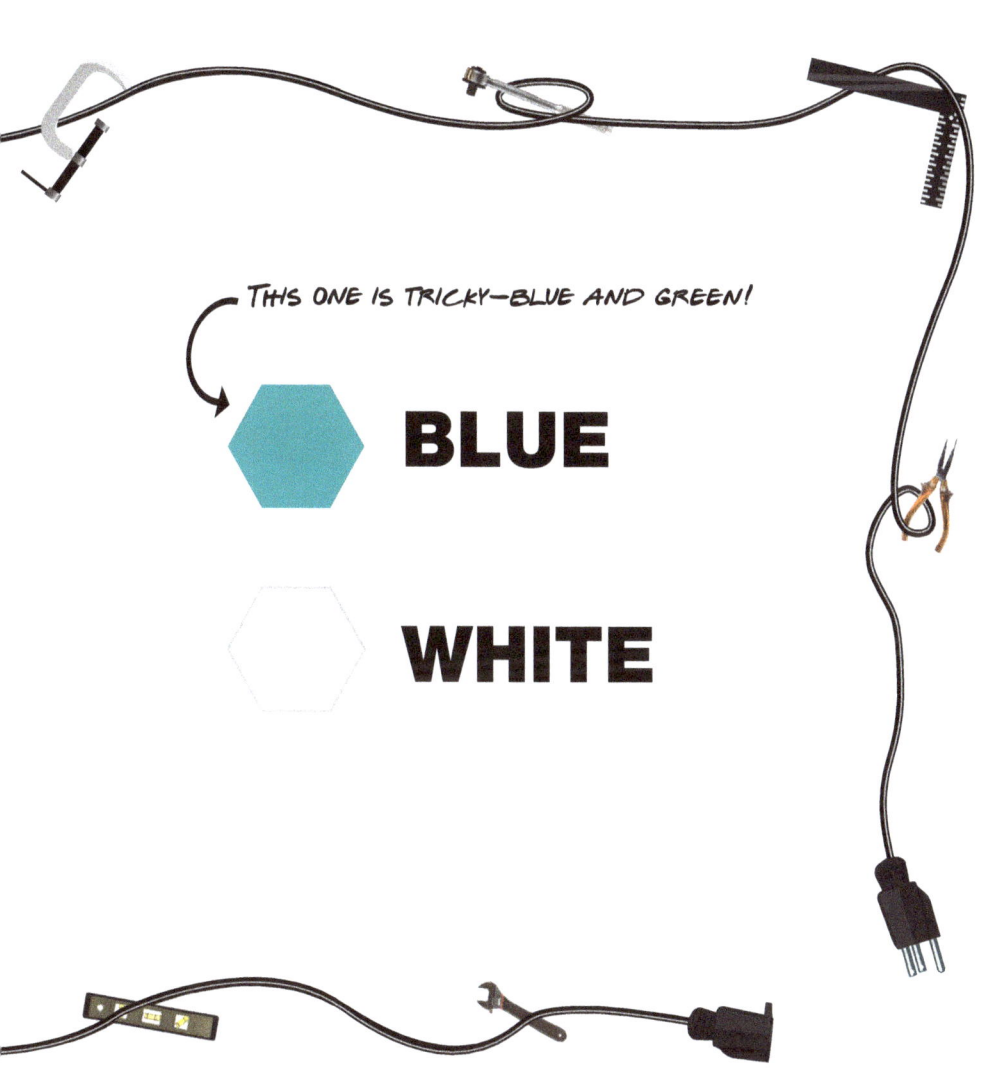

THIS ONE IS TRICKY—BLUE AND GREEN!

BLUE

WHITE

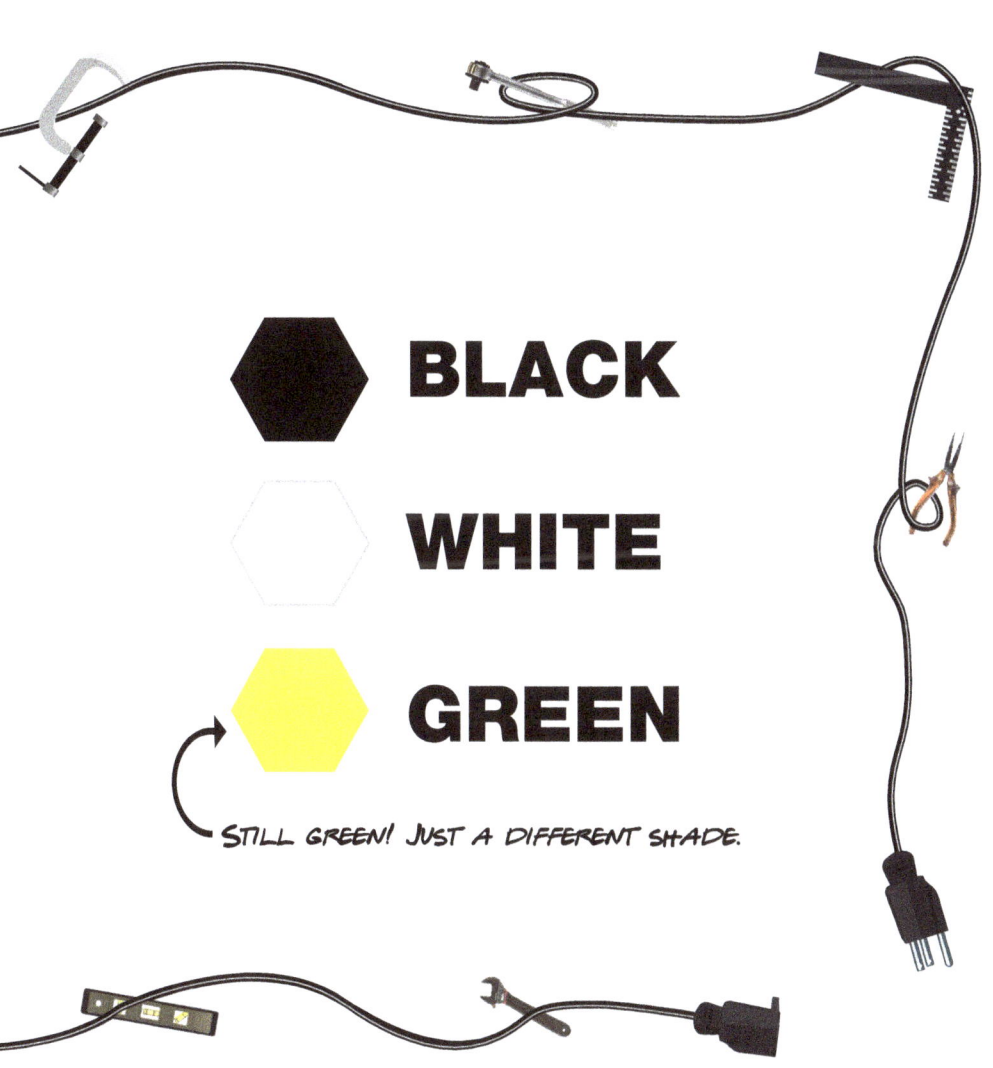

BLACK

WHITE

GREEN

STILL GREEN! JUST A DIFFERENT SHADE.

Claw Hammer

Groove-Joint Pliers

Speed Square

Combination Wrench

Torpedo Level

Framing Square

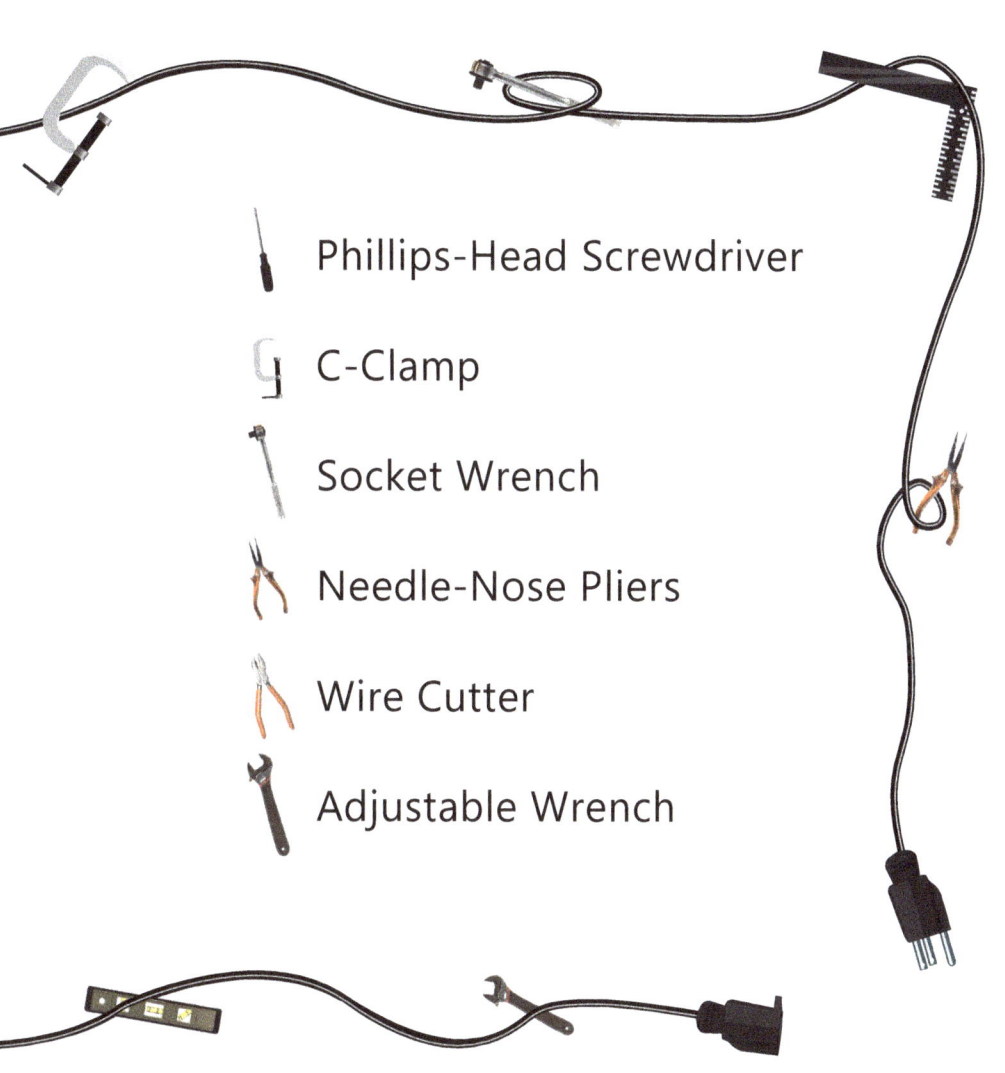

Phillips-Head Screwdriver

C-Clamp

Socket Wrench

Needle-Nose Pliers

Wire Cutter

Adjustable Wrench

Also Available